AMAZON IN PERIL

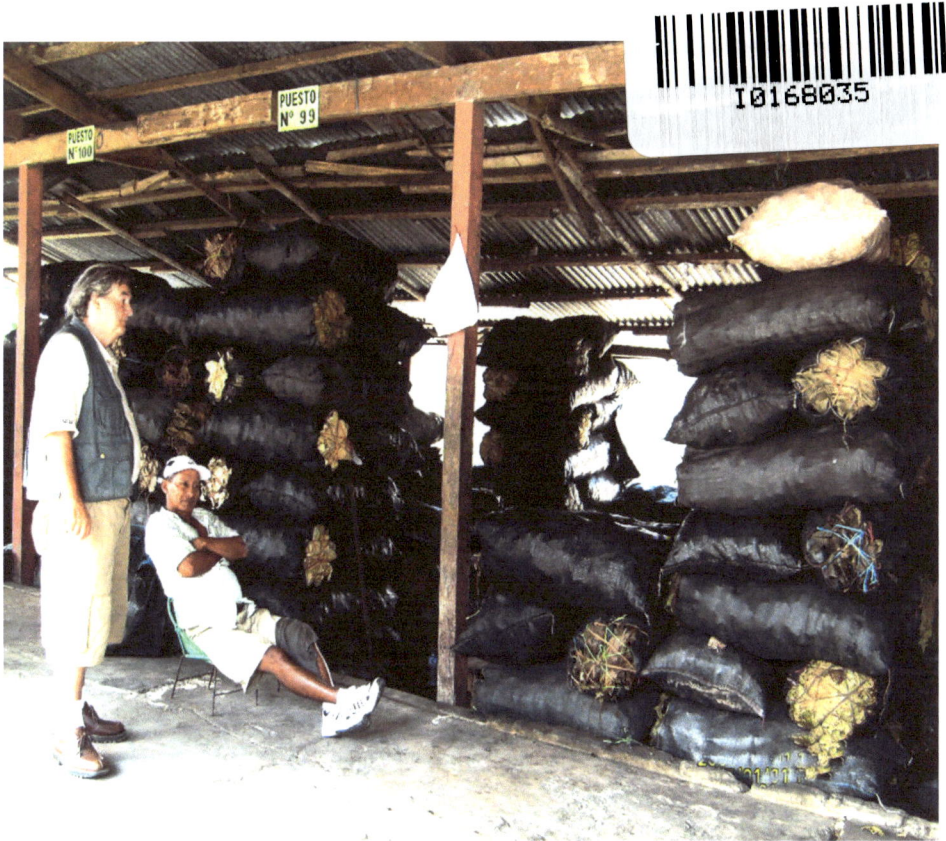

NORTHWATER

CONSTANTINE ISSIGHOS

NorthWater is an imprint of Awaqkuna Books Inc.

Vol. 18 Of THE AMAZON EXPLORATION SERIES:
AMAZON IN PERIL

Library and Archives Canada

ISBN ISBN 978-0-9878601-7-0

Library and Archives Canada Cataloguing in Publication

ATTENTION CHILDRENS ASSOCIATIONS, BOOK STORES, PUBLIC OR PRIVATE LIBRARIES: quantity discounts are available on bulk purchases of this book series.

THE AMAZON EXPLORATION SERIES
Children's Books
by
Constantine Issighos

The Amazon rainforest has often been described as an ancient ecosystem—a cradle of natural evolution. Its stable climate has allowed it to evolve slowly, which is evident by the fantastic biodiversity present today. Environmentalists, however, and organizations such as the Greenpeace, are concerned with the possible dramatic effects that global climate change may have upon the fragile Amazon ecosystem.

The Amazon rainforest has a long history of environmental destruction. In the last 500 years, since the time of the European conquest and settlement, the Amazon has been invaded by outsiders and outside economic interests.

Portuguese and Spanish Jesuits, and much later Protestant fundamentalists, in the name of religion and blessed by popes and heads of churches, began the long tradition of human abuse against the indigenous people, one that would be continued by secular colonialists, rubber barons, tappers, land developers, gold miners, hardwood loggers, oil companies, charcoal makers, illegal cocaine drug producers and agro-industrialists of life-stock and soya beans.

One infamous example of human rights abuse against the Putamayo Indians was typified by the British-registered rubber company, Peruvian Amazon Company. This company was controlled by the rubber barons Julio Cesar Arana, who latter became a successful politician. A report was written 17 March, 1911, by Sir Roger Casement; who witnessed the plight of the indigenous tappers, describing it as follows,

"Men, women, and children were confined in them stocks (confines) for days, weeks, and often months…Whole families…were imprisoned – fathers, mothers, and children, and many cases were reported of parents dying thus, either from starvation or from wounds caused by flogging while their offspring were attached alongside of them to watch in misery themselves the dying agonies of their parents"

Such vivid description of human rights abuse did not received well by the British business establishment. Segments of Sir Casement's report were circulated as part of a smear campaign against him in his latter trial (and his subsequent execution on 3 August 1916) as an Irish rebel.

Today, the indigenous plight has become an international battle among environmentalists, human rights activists, the government and the unscrupulous commercial industries. Indigenous social groups have mobilized and have developed an organizational base, forming united ethnic fronts as a way to protect themselves, their culture and their natural resources. One of the more pro-active indigenous tribes is the *Ashanikas,*

The *Ashanikas* people who are proud of their culture, driven by a strong sense of freedom, and mistrustful of governments, are always ready to stand up to invaders of their traditional lands. The *Ashanikas* tribal land is divided between the national territories of Brazil and Peru. It is a vast territory, extending from the right bank of the Elvira River of Brazil to the watersheds of the Andean mountain range of Peru.

The history of the Ashanikas did not begin with the arrival of the Europeans. They have lived in the Peruvian Selva Central (Central Jungle) for at least 5,000 years. The history of contact between the Ashanikas and non-Indians varies according to the region. Some Ashanikas groups have been in continuous contact since the 16th century, while others only since the end of the 19th century.

Simultaneously with the arrival of the colonialists in 1595, the Christian Jesuits also arrived, determined to "save" the indigenous by forcefully converting them to Christianity. For centuries, torture and fear-inducing religious superstitions and practices were widely used as a means of "salvation."

In 1635 the Franciscan Jesuits arrived in Ashanikas territory to begin an evangelical mission on the site of the present city of La Merced. By 1647, lured by the widespread myth of cities made of gold, an expedition of missionaries and mercenaries from La Merced tried to reach Cerro de la Sal—Hill of Salt—but they were decimated upon entering the Ashanikas land.

Foreign intrusions of Amazonian indigenous cultures have caused internal rivalries and conflicts which include challenges to Christian ideal. One of these was the indigenous practice of the chief's polygamy, which the monks and missionaries regarded as an example of scandalous social behaviour representing chaotic and primitive promiscuity.

Under this hostile religious influence, many indigenous groups live in fear of practicing their own traditional spiritual beliefs. Such foreign control continues today in many parts of the Amazon rainforest. The latest was in the 1960s when the New Tribal Mission, a fanatical Evangelical group, provoked tribal groups to go to war against each other. Indigenous people needed to kill each other, in order for them to learn the Christian command "Do not kill."

Throughout the following decades, the major missions were able to group together hundreds of indigenous families. Many of them subsequently fled and were replaced by others. Many families, generally through the chief's orders, remained with the missions to obtain metal tools and other goods.

Throughout the Amazon rainforest, indigenous groups, including the Ashanikas were displaced from their traditional lands and incorporated into newly developing lands so they could work on coffee plantations, and in the rubber and logging economies.

Many indigenous groups preferred to live in isolation, cultivating their lands with traditional crops such as corn (maize), bananas, yucca, sweet potatoes and more. In the interior of the Amazon, towards the Andean mountain range, one of the most traditional crops is the coca plant.

The coca plant has been part of the indigenous culture for millennia. It is used for traditional ceremonies, as well as for its proven healing qualities. The leaves of the coca plant contain energy-inducing ingredients that help a person's respiratory system, especially important for those who live in the extremely high elevations of the Andean range where the oxygen level is low. Coca leaves can be used in a variety of forms such as tea (coca tea) and in energy drinks. In fact, until 1905, Coca Cola drinks contained extracts of coca ingredients in order to enhance their flavour. Today, the Coca Cola Co. in order to maintain its trade mark "Coca Cola" still contain in its drinks .5ml of coca ingredients, otherwise known as cocaine. Coca Cola still uses .5ml de-cocainized leaves (chemically processed) as one of its main flavours, as well as Arabic Gum. Most energy drinks, such as Red Bull and others, contain the legally permitted .5ml quantity of cocaine. One point to remember is this: coca leaves are not equivalent to cocaine.

The so called "drug war" in the Amazon jungle is about the eradication of the coca plant, the chemically process of coca leaves and the sale of its final product: cocaine.

The powerful drug cartels of Peru, Colombia and Bolivia have invaded the Amazon rainforest to set up illegal chemical laboratories that process the coca leaves. The end result is to extract its benzoylmethylecgonine, the powerful and addictive psychotropic drug known as cocaine.

The illegal laboratories need large quantities of water to process the coca plants. This is why most of them are located close to the rivers, tributaries and streams of the Amazon. During the chemical process, large quantities of coca leaves are soaked in chemical baths of kerosene, sulphuric acid and other contaminants. When the chemical process is completed, all these powerful chemical contaminants are disposed of into the rivers, tributaries and streams, killing many freshwater species. These chemicals are not easily absorbed by nature; they will continue to destroy the Amazon's fragile ecosystem for many years. They put the health of the Amazon, including the health of thousands of indigenous families and their children, in peril. This is not all!

In the last 50 years, there has been an ongoing war between the narco-traffickers, mercenaries and soldiers of the various nations bordering the Amazon basin. Caught between these fighting forces are the indigenous cocaleros, coca farmers, who are forcefully intimidated by the army who destroy their crop, kill their livestock and destroy their livelihood.

The drug cartels of Peru, Bolivia and Colombia and their paid national and foreign mercenaries force the indigenous cocaleros to move further and further into the Amazon jungle to avoid detection from search-and-destroy anti-drug forces. In this vicious process, the lives of the indigenous people are destroyed and their family members are dispersed to different parts of the country. Live-stocks is left behind, along with the elders, who cannot travel the treacherous terrain of the Amazon basin. Under these conditions, life for the indigenous people can be described as being vicious, nasty, brutish and short!

There is a new secular "evangelical" period which is taking place. It is mainly guided by economic and political interest, rather than religious or "civilizing" concerns. Neo-colonialism is encouraged by government policies to facilitate the interests of powerful trans-national corporations. Through migration incentives, hundreds of thousands of coffee and banana plantation labourers, rubber tappers and gold miners were transplanted onto indigenous lands under the pretext of "development." The Ashanikas and the Yunomani were steadily incorporated as labourers or gathered into neo-economic colonies. Little by little these indigenous people began to lose their identity due to growing presence of the non-indigenous migrants and their lifestyle. However, the Ashanikas tribe along the borders of Peru and Brazil and the Yanomani tribe along the borders of Bra-zil and Venezuela have a long history of resistance, of standing up against invaders of their ancestral lands. They have resisted the des-tructiveness of the loggers, charcoal makers, gold miners, oil com-panies and large agro-businesses that have tried to pollute and des-troy their traditional territories.

Progressively, indigenous protection activities gathered strength in the mid-1980s at the height of the logging of mahogany hardwood and the gold miners' mercury pollution of watersheds. The cost of the environmental restoration became the battle cry of the indige-nous people. Their battle was physical as well as legal.

The indigenous shamanistic cosmological traditions were awakened by the people's involvement in the messianic declaration of revolu-tionary movements. The Ashanikas of Peru, out of sheer reaction to their dreadful social conditions, joined the rank and file of the Left-wing Revolutionary Movement—Movimiento de Isquierta Revolu-cionaria—(MIR), in the mid-1960s. In the mid-1980s, following the guidance of a powerful shaman, some Ashanikas groups saw the MIR as the return of Itomi Pawa—Son of God—and the hope for a better future.

The Yanomani formed armed bands and conducted war battles against the gold miners and loggers who were out to kill any indigenous people who interfered with their gold mining and logging interests. Gold mining corporations armed individual gold miners with specific orders to shoot and kill any indigenous protestors as a condition for the purchase of the miner's gold.

Between 1965 and 1990, in the Ecuadorian Amazon, the oil and gas giant Texaco dumped more than 18 billion gallons of toxic waste into the waterways, and over 900 waste pits still overflow waste into the streams. The Huarani tribal people and their leaders are not only involved in violent confrontations with loggers of balsa wood, but are also in legal court battles against the Chevron and Texaco oil and gas polluters.

This is the final narrative of my Amazon Exploration Series. It has been an incredible learning experience living for a number of years in South America, including in the Amazon Rainforest and amongst the native communities of the Andean Sierras.

I am humbled by the awesomeness of the Amazon rainforest, the power of the life and death cycle, and the diversity of its animal species and inhabitants. I am satisfied that I have honestly tried to present a true picture of its biodiversity, of the raw beauty of its sunrises and landscapes, of its powerful rainstorms and of the inherited dangers that are part of the Amazon environment. I am not sure whether I have achieved my task. I am willing, however, to accept your judgement as to the success or shortcomings of my photo narratives.

AMAZON CHARCOAL MAKERS

PEOPLE's PROTEST

LOGGING IN AMAZON

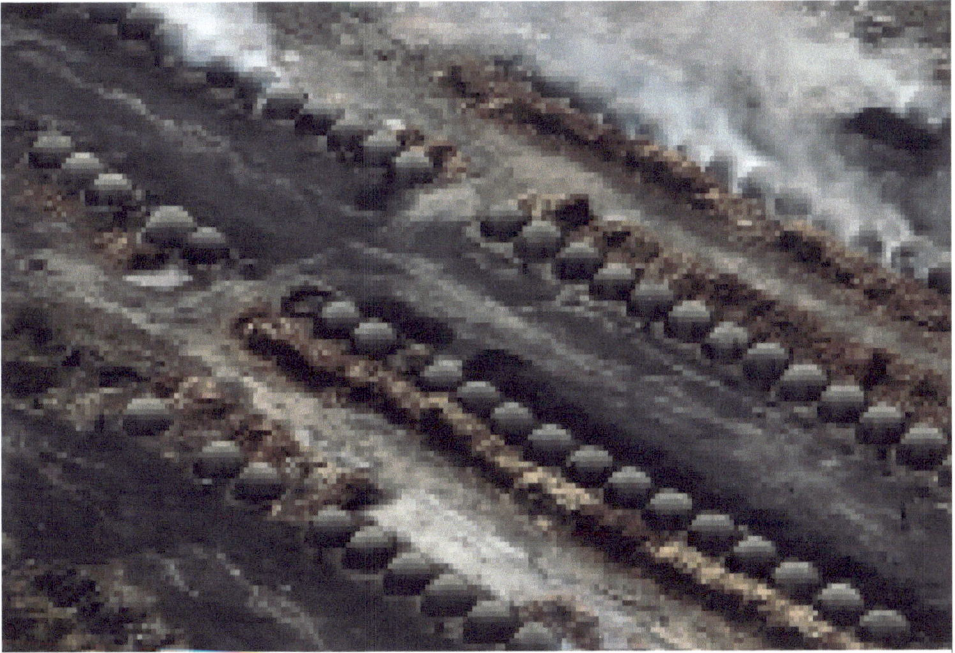

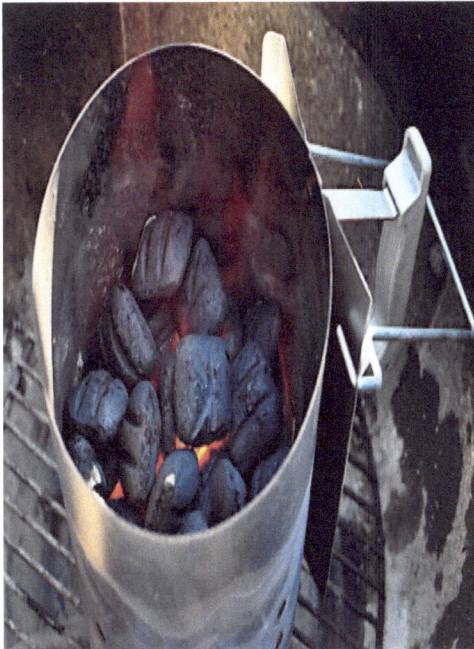

www.ingramcontent.com/pod-product-compliance
Lightning Source LLC
Chambersburg PA
CBHW041530090426
42738CB00035B/26